2

D1124114

Date and Acquaintance Rape

Perspectives on Violence

by Gus Gedatus

Consultant:
Christopher James Sorensen, MSW
School Violence Prevention Program Coordinator
Harriet Tubman Center
Minneapolis, Minnesota

LifeMatters
an imprint of Capstone Press
Mankato, Minnesota

LifeMatters Books are published by Capstone Press
PO Box 669 • 151 Good Counsel Drive • Mankato, Minnesota 56002
http://www.capstone-press.com

Printed in the United States of America

Library of Congress Cataloging-in-Publication Data

Gedatus, Gustav Mark.
     Date and acquaintance rape / by Gus Gedatus.
          p. cm. — (Perspectives on violence)
     Includes bibliographical references and index.
     Summary: Describes what rape is, some causes of date or acquaintance rape, the effects of this crime, and steps to deal with and prevent it.
     ISBN 0-7368-0424-2 (book) — ISBN 0-7368-0439-0 (series)
     1. Acquaintance rape—Juvenile literature. [1. Acquaintance rape. 2. Rape. 3. Dating violence.] I. Title. II. Series
     HV6558.G43 2000
     362.883—dc21
                                                99-054211
                                            CIP

Staff Credits

Anne Heller, Charles Pederson, editors; Adam Lazar, designer; Jodi Theisen, photo researcher

Photo Credits

Cover: The Stock Market/©T & D McCarthy, large; ©Roy McMahon, small
FPG/©Ron Chapple, 13; ©John Lawlor, 48
Index Stock Imagery, 25
International Stock/©Scott Barrow, 20; ©Giovanni Lunardi, 27; ©Michael Paras, 57; ©Jay Thomas, 58
Photo Network/©T. J. Florian, 31; ©Esbin-Anderson, 47
Unicorn/©Dennis MacDonald, 28
Uniphoto/©Lew Lause, 16; ©Bob Daemmrich, 35; ©Jim Schafer, 53

A 0 9 8 7 6 5 4 3 2 1

Table of Contents

Rape is any forced, unwanted sexual intercourse with another person. It is a crime of power over the victim.

Date and acquaintance rape is forced sexual intercourse with someone known to the victim.

The number of reported rapes has been dropping. Many cases of rape, especially date and acquaintance rape, are not reported to authorities. The victim is *never* to blame for the attack.

Most people who commit date rape seem like ordinary people.

A person's consent to sexual activity may change.

Chapter 1

What Is Date and Acquaintance Rape?

Most teens date. Dating is a fun way to get to know other people. It is exciting to find out about others and to let them find out about you. Dating is a normal and enjoyable part of becoming an adult. Unfortunately, some dating situations might not be safe. This book is meant to help you learn how to keep yourself safe on dates and with acquaintances.

What Is Date and Acquaintance Rape?

Broadly, rape is any unwanted, forced sexual intercourse with someone. Rape is an act of violence, or words and actions that hurt people or the things they care about. Some attackers are strangers who rape and then disappear. Most people who commit rape, however, are people known to their victims. They may be friends, neighbors, classmates, or dates.

Forced sexual intercourse with someone the victim knows is called date rape or acquaintance rape. Sexual activity among people who are closely related is called incest. This topic is not covered in this book. The force used can come from threats or tone of voice as well as from physical power or weapons. Date rape, like rape by a stranger, is a serious violent crime. It is about gaining power over a person rather than a desire for sex.

FAST FACT

Most rapists, or people who commit rape, are male. Most rape victims are female, though males can be victims of rape, too. Most of the safety measures described in this book apply to both males and females.

How Often Does Rape Occur?

Recent statistics show positive news. The number of reported rapes decreased steadily between 1992 and 1999. Reported rapes recently dropped to their lowest number in 15 years. Experts believe that as people become more sensitive to the problem of rape, the number will continue dropping.

Unreported Rape

More rape victims seem willing to report rape today than those in the past. However, date and acquaintance rape often goes unreported. Various estimates show that 50 to 90 percent of victims do not report date rape to police. Victims may hesitate because no weapon or physical violence was involved. A victim may be afraid of not being believed. A victim may have consented, or agreed, to have sex with the person in the past. As a result, some victims may feel responsible for the rape or embarrassed about it. It's important to remember that the victim is *never* responsible for being raped.

"I used to feel better about myself each time I had sex with another date. I thought that meant one more person found me attractive. One day I realized that I was using females to boost my own ego. I now know I was acting selfish and immature."—Sean, age 18

Because many rapes are not reported, experts don't have an accurate idea of how often these crimes really occur. The American Medical Association (AMA) estimates that 700,000 people are victims of sexual assault every year. Assault is violence that can cause permanent physical and emotional harm, yet that may not be fatal. The AMA's estimate of sexual assaults includes rape by strangers as well as by people known to victims. The National Victim Center estimates that about 30 percent of rapes happen to females ages 11 to 17. Some agencies estimate that more than 70 percent of rape victims know their attacker.

Those Who Rape

Most people who commit date or acquaintance rape are ordinary people. Most of them don't look or act any differently from other people. They usually do not have a police record of violent behavior.

Rapists' feelings of self-worth often are linked closely to their sexual success with their victim. Many people who have admitted committing date rape say that they had planned to have sex with their dates.

Myth: Rapes are unplanned acts that occur in dark alleys and are committed by strangers.

Fact: About 82 percent of rapes are planned beforehand. More than 70 percent of victims know their rapist.

CORY, AGE 18

Cory and two friends have a "babe" club. Their goal is to have sex with more females than their friends do. The losers pay a hundred dollars to the one with the highest "babe count." So far this year, Cory has gone all the way with four girls. His friend Jeff has had sex with five girls, and his friend James, with two.

"I doubt you'll get your way with Jennifer," Jeff warned. "I don't know anyone who has gotten her to say yes."

"We'll see about that. I have an idea she'll go along with what I want," said Cory.

"Are you going to trap her or make her feel like she owes you?" asked James. The three guys laughed and then went off to class.

Setting Up the Rape

Some date or acquaintance rapes are unplanned. The attacker may be able to take advantage of an opportunity that happens to occur. For example, no one else may be in a house with an attacker and a victim. The attacker may take that as a chance to rape the victim.

Many attackers do plan beforehand to have sex. Attackers who plan a sexual encounter may meet the victim in a place where escape is difficult. They may describe plans that include other people. Then, the victim may be surprised to find that the plans no longer include those people. In some cases, attackers give their victim alcohol or other drugs. The victim may then lose self-control and engage in sex that normally would not occur. The alcohol or drugs may make the victim unconscious and helpless against the rape.

Myth: If the victim isn't a virgin, it's not really rape.

Fact: If either party does not consent to having sex, then it becomes rape, even if the victim is not a virgin.

Gang Rapes

Occasionally, an acquaintance rape may turn into a gang rape. This happens when more than one attacker rapes someone. Gang rapes often occur at parties. Both the attackers and the victim may have been using alcohol or other drugs. This sort of rape may or may not start out with the victim agreeing to have sex with one person. Others who see this sexual activity might assume that the victim should willingly have sex with them, too. In this type of rape, the victim knows about one-third of the attackers.

Often, people who participate in gang rape would not otherwise take advantage of another person this way. However, they may give in to peer pressure. They may feel they must prove themselves to friends who are participating. This sort of activity can quickly get out of control. This is especially true if alcohol or other drugs are being used.

Rape by a partner differs from rape by a stranger in that it is likely to occur repeatedly.

When a Person's Consent Changes

Usually, couples have sex when both people consent. This sex is not forced. However, what was okay in the past may not be okay in the present. For example, one partner may decide that sex is no longer a good idea. Maybe a dating relationship comes to an end. When these things happen, neither partner can expect to continue having sex with the other person.

Once either partner says no to sex, the sex should end. Setting clear boundaries for oneself about how much sexual activity to take part in is important. Knowing these physical and emotional limits and communicating them to a partner makes it easier for people to say no. Chapter 4 talks more about setting boundaries.

Points to Consider

Why do you think most rape happens between people who know each other?

Why do you think the number of reported rapes has dropped in recent years?

What could you do to stop a gang rape?

Do you think that feeling embarrassed is a good reason not to report being raped? Why or why not?

Chapter
Overview

Chapter
Overview

People from all backgrounds can be victims of date rape.

Mistaken ideas and poor communication can lead to rape.

Alcohol and other drug use can change the way people behave. This may lead to date and acquaintance rape.

Chapter 2

Causes of Date and Acquaintance Rape

Date and acquaintance rape has many causes. Some attackers make excuses as to why they commit rape. However, there is no excuse for rape. Remember: No matter what might happen before a rape, the victim is *never* responsible. The attacker is solely responsible for the rape.

Rapes happen to people of all ethnic, racial, and religious groups. They happen to rich people as well as poor people. Why do they happen? Experts believe date and acquaintance rape occurs for a number of reasons. Among the reasons are poor communication and wrong ideas, as well as alcohol and other drug use.

Trisha had always wanted to go
out with Robbie. He was a nice

guy and a great jazz guitar player. Almost everyone in school
knew him and liked him. However, when Trisha finally went
out with Robbie, he raped her in his car.

Trisha asked her parents to call the police. After Robbie was
arrested, the police notified school officials. Everyone heard
about what had happened.

"Robbie has had sex with lots of girls. Do you think they all
wanted to do it with him? No way," said a girl named Rita.
"But at least they kept their mouth shut like they're supposed
to. They didn't go and get him in trouble afterward."

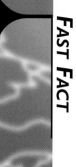
About 12 percent of teenage girls and 20 percent of adult women in the United States have been raped.

Poor Communication and Mistaken Ideas

Rape sometimes happens because of poor communication and wrong ideas that people have. Rita believes that girls should not get an acquaintance in trouble for rape. This is one example of a mistaken idea that someone might have. Robbie may believe that he can get away with rape, because his victims will never turn him in. Miscommunication or believing wrong ideas is no excuse for rape. There is never an excuse.

The following are some examples of wrong ideas or poor communication. Notice in each case that it is the attacker's choice to rape the victim. No one asks or deserves to be raped.

> The victim may agree to be alone with the attacker. The attacker may wrongly believe that this means the victim wants to have sex. The attacker doesn't ask if this is the victim's intention.

"Hey, guys. Let me ask you something. Would you kill someone to have sex? No? Then don't rape anyone, because that is almost as bad as killing them."
—Treena, age 25, raped at age 16

The victim may wear clothing that the attacker sees as sexy. The attacker may think this means the victim is asking for sex. However, the attacker may not ask the victim if this is what she or he means. They may fail to communicate their beliefs to each other.

Both people may believe that the other owes something if one person pays for a date. That something may be sex.

The victim may not clearly explain what she or he wants. The attacker may believe this means the victim wants to have sex.

A victim may say no to sex. The attacker may believe the victim is playing hard to get. The attacker may feel challenged to talk or force the victim into having sex.

People are more vulnerable to date rape than to stranger rape for these reasons:

They trust their attacker before the rape.

They may not realize right away what is happening.

They may not want to fight their attacker for fear of embarrassing themselves or someone they know.

They may be using alcohol or other drugs.

The attacker may know that the victim has had sex with other people and feel challenged to have sex, too. The attacker doesn't communicate with the victim about limits.

Some victims may have learned that they are supposed to be polite. They may worry that saying what they want may seem too bold or offensive to their date. The attacker may believe that because the victim doesn't object, it's okay to have sex.

Alcohol and Other Drug Use

Alcohol and other drugs often play an important part in date rape. In fact, some experts believe that 75 percent of rapists drink or take drugs before raping. More than half of all victims use alcohol or other drugs before being raped.

The behavior of the victim, attacker, or both may change when they drink alcohol or take other drugs. In many cases, attackers become more sexually aggressive.

Victims may lose their self-control and agree to have sex when they normally would not. In spite of this agreement, victims can still press charges of rape against their attacker. Agreeing to have sex while under the influence of alcohol or other drugs is not considered legal consent.

The victim also may pass out while using alcohol or other drugs. If unconscious, the victim cannot consent to having sex. Without consent, any sex with the victim is rape, which is a crime.

Date and Acquaintance Rape

Rohypnol, often called "roofies," is an illegal sedative. It is sometimes called the date rape drug. It may be given to victims to knock them out and make them helpless against rape.

Points to Consider

Do you think Trisha did the right thing by calling police after Robbie raped her? Why or why not?

Why is good communication important when people are on a date?

What are some situations that could put a person at risk for date rape?

Why do you think people use alcohol and other drugs if that use leads so often to rape?

Rape usually has serious emotional effects on victims.

Victims may have physical problems that last for a long time.

Rape victims may have trouble with future sexual relationships. They may have trouble sharing their emotional pain with others.

Attackers' lives may be changed forever after they rape someone.

A victim is *never* to blame for rape.

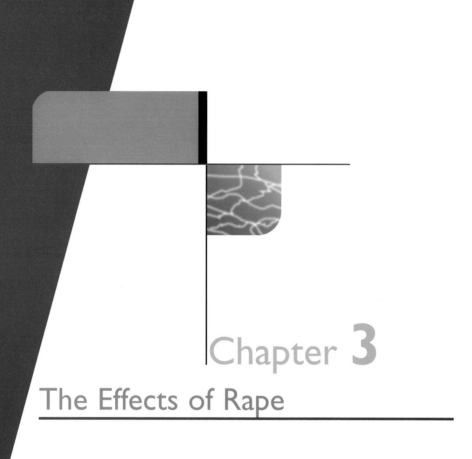

Chapter **3**

The Effects of Rape

Rape is a violent crime that can affect the victim in many ways. The emotional damage is tremendous. The victim's physical health and sexual relationships may be harmed as well.

Emotional Effects

Each victim has different feelings about being raped. Some victims fear being alone. Such fear can last for a long time. Some victims go through denial. They try to believe the rape did not happen.

"I felt as if my whole world was turned upside down."—Lynn, age 19, raped by a neighbor

CALVERT, AGE 18, AND DARCIE, AGE 17

Darcie's parents were gone and Darcie was bored, so she accepted Calvert's invitation for a date. When Calvert brought her home, Darcie simply wanted to thank him and say good night. She hoped he would leave. Instead, he followed her to the door. She said good night again, but he insisted on coming in. Calvert knew Darcie was alone, and he raped her.

As soon as Calvert left, Darcie wondered what to do. She was shaking and felt afraid to be alone. She also felt embarrassed and like she was to blame. She kept wondering if somehow she had caused the rape. Since her parents were gone, she finally decided to call the police.

When the police arrived, an officer questioned Darcie about what had happened. The officer was supportive and told Darcie she was not to blame. She said Darcie needed to get to the hospital for an exam. She asked if Darcie wanted to press charges against Calvert. All Darcie wanted to do was forget the whole thing. She felt like she might go crazy facing Calvert again, even if it was in court.

Victims of rape often feel angry with their attacker. In many cases, the victim feels angry with himself or herself. The victim may think some wrong decision caused the rape. It's important to keep remembering that nothing the victim did caused the rape.

At times, the victim may feel embarrassed or anxious. She or he may not be ready to relive the experience by talking about it. At other times, the victim may need to talk about what happened. When ready, a victim can talk with a friend, family member, or professional counselor. Support groups also help survivors of rape deal with their experience. The Useful Addresses and Internet Sites section on page 62 lists other sources of help for victims of rape.

When the rapist is a stranger, the victim may feel that friends and family will provide support and protection. However, when a victim knows the attacker, that feeling of support and safety may vanish. The victim may feel as though no one can be trusted. The situation may be even more complicated if the victim and the rapist share friends. The victim may feel alone in coping with the effects of the rape.

Physical Effects

Physical problems can result from rape. A victim could get a sexually transmitted disease, including human immunodeficiency virus (HIV). This is the virus that leads to AIDS. A female victim could become pregnant.

When extreme force is used, the victim may have serious damage to the genitals. These include the vagina, the penis, and other sexual organs. Other parts of the body may be seriously injured as well.

Long-term physical problems may arise from the emotional trauma of rape. Trauma is a severe physical or emotional shock or injury. For example, some victims have ongoing stomachaches, headaches, or back problems. Some have trouble concentrating or sleeping. Many rape victims have decreased appetite. Others may have eating disorders. Some victims may not eat enough, or they may overeat.

Sexual Effects

Some people who have been raped may fear having sex. They may be especially frightened of people who somehow resemble their attacker. Sex may make them feel angry or disgusted. It may make victims recall memories that they don't want to think about.

Rape victims who no longer trust other people may take years to develop a satisfying sexual relationship. Overcoming the mistrust may require a partner who is patient with the difficulties the victim has. The victim also may require therapy to overcome the mistrust.

Difficulties in Sharing the Hurt

After being raped, a victim may get valuable emotional support from family members and friends. However, victims of acquaintance rape may fear telling loved ones what has happened. They may fear that loved ones cannot handle it. Victims may feel at risk of being judged. The fact is, victims usually are believed, especially by their family and friends.

Occasionally, boyfriends or girlfriends may not understand. They may blame the victim, or their feelings about the victim may change. Sometimes, an acquaintance rape may raise questions or doubts that cause the end of a close relationship. Though untrue, the boyfriend or girlfriend may wonder if the victim enjoyed the experience. He or she may wonder if the victim was cheating. He or she may believe that the victim could have resisted if that person had wanted to.

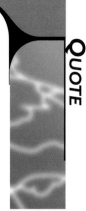
"Saying victims cause rape is like saying banks cause robberies. No one deserves to be raped."
—Alice Vachss, teacher, counselor, and lawyer

In some cases, family members and friends may not understand. If the rapist is someone the family knows, the victim's friends may challenge the claims of rape. Parents or others sometimes pass judgment on the victim because of their own hurt or confused feelings. In some cases, religious beliefs affect people's attitudes and cause them to judge the victim harshly.

All these things may make victims not want to tell what happened to them. However, victims always need to talk with someone about the attack.

Consequences for the Attacker

Someone who is arrested for date rape may face many consequences. The arrest may create embarrassment and hurt for the attacker's family. The attacker may face time in prison, in a work release program, or on probation. An arrest may delay future school and career plans. A criminal record can seriously affect the attacker's future job opportunities. A pattern of abusive behavior may decrease the attacker's chances of building healthy relationships in the future.

"When I was released from my one-year prison term for rape, people treated me like an outcast. And worse than that, I know I will never get over the feeling that what I did was selfish and just plain evil. If I ever have a daughter, how will I feel, looking into her eyes, after what I have done?"—Damon, age 19, who raped a girl on their second date

Rape Is Never Justified

Occasionally, when one person accuses another person of rape, people blame the victim. They may feel that the victim's behavior justified what happened. Such beliefs are wrong. No rape victim is ever to blame for what has happened. Chapter 2 lists many wrong ideas people might hold about rape.

Unfortunately, a rape victim, too, may believe some of these ideas. The victim may feel that he or she caused the rape. This is wrong. The victim is never to blame.

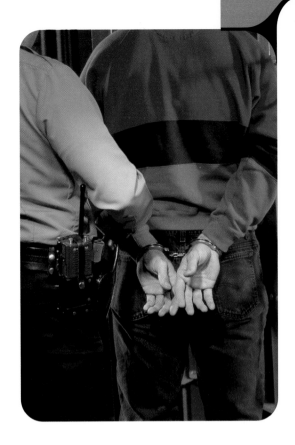

Points to Consider

When Calvert raped Darcie, she couldn't decide what to do next. What do you think Darcie should have done?

How do you think rape might affect a person?

If a friend told you he or she had been raped by someone you both know, how would you react?

Do you think rape more seriously affects the victim or the attacker? Explain.

Setting clear boundaries is an important part of taking care of yourself.

Many people who rape have common characteristics.

Communication between dating partners is important both before and during a date.

Acquaintance rape can be avoided in nondating situations.

Chapter 4

Protecting Yourself From Date and Acquaintance Rape

Setting Clear Boundaries

Most people have boundaries for being close to others. For example, a physical boundary is the space you keep between yourself and another person when talking. You may require more distance with strangers than with close friends. Physical boundaries may change, depending on your mood or emotional state.

Myth: A female who goes somewhere alone with a male wants to have sex with him.

Fact: Two people can be alone with one another for many reasons that have nothing to do with sex. Unless the female consents to sex, it is rape.

Your emotional boundaries may vary with different people. For example, you may allow your sister to say something to you that you would not accept from a stranger. Sexually suggestive comments from an acquaintance may violate one of your emotional boundaries.

Once you have identified your boundaries, it's important to tell others what they are. Ask that others respect your boundaries, and expect that they will do so. If someone does not respect your boundaries, tell the person. For example, you might say, "Mr. Smith, you seem like a nice man. But please don't touch me when you say hello. Not my arm, not my shoulder, not anywhere."

You can be polite and direct. You do not have to embarrass or put down the person. In keeping boundaries, notice your body language and eye contact. Does your appearance match what you are saying or feeling? They should match if the other person is to get the message correctly. For example, in talking with Mr. Smith, you would have a serious expression and speak loudly and clearly. You would look Mr. Smith directly in the eye. You wouldn't smile or giggle.

Young people sometimes have trouble enforcing their boundaries. Even if you are clear and direct, always tell another adult who can help you.

Date and Acquaintance Rape

James was a football player and a straight-A student. He had never been on a date because he was usually busy studying and practicing. His friends frequently bragged about how often they had sex. James felt so out of it because he didn't really want to have sex.

JAMES, AGE 17

When James asked Diedre to go out, he didn't tell her she was his first real date. What would she expect? What would they do when they were alone?

"I was a little nervous going out with you," Diedre explained to James when he said good-bye. "I have heard about how so many football players are all over a girl on the first date. Just know that if you want to see me again, don't push for sex at all. I won't have anyone touch me until I am ready."

James was relieved. He liked Diedre, and knowing her boundaries took off any pressure to try to have sex. It gave him a chance to concentrate on getting to know her.

In a study of college students, 75 percent of women who were raped did not realize it at the time. About 1 in 12 men admitted having forced someone to have sex. Almost none of these men considered themselves rapists.

Spotting a Potential Rapist

It helps to be able to spot people who may be rapists. Many people who assault their dates have some common traits. As you get to know a new person, be cautious if you see some of these behaviors. A potential rapist may:

Ignore what you have to say, including when you say no

Seem to enjoy putting you down, especially in front of others

Seem to show anger toward people of your gender in general

Insist on making all of the decisions

Try to make you feel guilty or uptight about sex

Seem possessive or jealous

Seem to believe that females are meant for males' use

Use alcohol or other drugs that can cause big changes in the way the potential rapist treats you

"Dating is mostly about talking. You have to talk to get to know someone. Then you will have a better chance to know how this person thinks and whether you want to see him again."—Kim, age 15

Protecting Yourself on a Date

Dating is an important part of being a teen. It can be a lot of fun. However, it also is important to think ahead about protecting yourself. Only you can decide what makes you comfortable or uncomfortable. Once you know what these things are, communicate them to your date. The following ideas can help you have positive dating experiences.

Before You Date Someone

Ask others about how the person treats dating partners.

Tell someone where you are going and when you expect to return.

Help decide where you will go and what you will do. Don't leave it all up to your date.

Think about your attitudes toward money. Will you feel obligated if your date pays for the evening?

Offer to go on a double date or group date if you feel uncertain about dating someone alone. It is perfectly okay to turn down a date, too.

Decide on your boundaries for sexual activity.

Myth: When males become sexually aroused, they can't stop themselves from forcing a female to have sex.

Fact: Males are always able to control themselves, even after becoming sexually excited.

When on a Date

Communicate your boundaries clearly to dating partners.

Go on a date in a public place where other people are around.

Say no clearly and as if you mean it.

Follow your instincts if a dating situation doesn't feel right. Change the situation as soon as possible. For example, ask the person to leave your house, or get away to where other people are.

Keep enough money for cab fare or to call home.

If You Feel You Are in Danger of Being Raped

Lie if necessary. Tell the attacker you are going to throw up or that you have a sexually transmitted disease. If you are at your house, tell the attacker that family members will be home any minute.

Call it rape. Using the word *rape* may cool off some attackers.

Scream for help. This is no time for politeness.

If you are in a car, honk the horn if possible.

Punch or kick if you can. Aim for vulnerable areas such as the eyes, throat, or genitals.

Look for a way to stop an attacker, if only temporarily. Use your purse, a lamp, a tree branch, or some other object. However, do this as a last resort, as it could put you in greater danger.

JENNY, AGE 16

Jenny's friend Pam drove the two of them to a party. It was at the house of a boy whose parents were gone. The party was fun at first. It changed, however, as people started drinking. Jenny began to have a bad feeling.

Jenny got Pam, and they went to find Pam's car. A group of boys neither of them knew were hanging around Pam's car. The girls went back to the party so Jenny could call home. Her dad came within a few minutes. Together, they decided it was best to leave Pam's car overnight and go home with Jenny's dad.

Her dad didn't lecture her. He was glad to have helped her and Pam. Jenny knew that she had made the right decision.

After a person says no, any unwanted sexual behavior from another person is a crime.

Avoiding Rape in Nondating Situations

Some attackers are not dates. They may be family friends, neighbors, or coworkers. They may have intentions that could threaten you even if you aren't dating them. Here are some ideas to keep yourself safe in nondating situations.

Trust your instincts if a familiar person's interest in you gives you a funny feeling. Don't be alone with the person.

Tell the person when he or she has invaded your boundaries.

Tell the person that his or her sexually suggestive comments make you uncomfortable.

Tell the person to stop if you don't want his or her touches or kisses.

Threaten to notify police if the person seems to be following or stalking you. Follow through and call the police if the person doesn't stop following you.

Go with a friend if you are attending a party. Agree to watch out for one another.

Don't announce that you are walking home alone as you leave a party. Walk with another person or a group if possible.

Always have money with you for cab fare or to call home.

Points to Consider

What are your emotional boundaries? What are your physical boundaries?

How could you tell someone what your boundaries are?

What are the most important things you can do to protect yourself on a date? Why?

Chapter
Overview

Chapter
Overview

A victim of rape is *never* to blame.

Rape victims can take many steps to get help.

When someone you care about is raped, you can provide valuable support.

Being a good listener is the best way you can support a rape victim.

Chapter **5**

When You or Someone You Care About Is the Victim

Brett raped Vonda during her senior year. She said, "Afterward,

VONDA, AGE 18

I walked home, almost a mile and a half. I couldn't stop crying. When I got home I ripped off my clothes and threw every piece in the trash. I didn't want to see those clothes ever again."

Vonda tried to commit suicide two weeks later. The school counselor helped Vonda to get into regular counseling sessions.

Vonda said, "Counseling is good. I like my therapist. It's been really helpful to have someone who'll listen to me, someone who won't talk like it's my fault. It might take awhile, but I think I can get over this rape."

In a college survey, more than **80** percent of rape victims said the experience permanently changed them.

If You Are a Victim

No matter how careful a person is, rape sometimes still happens. If you are ever the victim of rape, here are some steps to take.

Remember that the rape is not your fault. You are not to blame.

Get to a clinic or hospital right away for immediate medical attention. Most medical centers have someone on staff who is trained to help victims of sexual assault.

Do not change your clothes and do not take a shower. This will preserve valuable evidence.

Hospital authorities may call the police, but you do not have to talk with them. It is the victim's decision whether to report a rape.

Consider whether you want to file charges against the attacker. Your parents or a social worker can help you decide whether to do this. A social worker can tell you what will happen if you press charges.

Get counseling to help deal with your feelings about the attack. The counseling center will explain your options for different kinds of counseling. Being with people who can identify with your pain can help you deal with the rape.

Seek out friends or family members who can give you continuing emotional support.

"I wanted to be alone and never talk with anyone about it. I didn't want to be accused of anything. I felt so ashamed."
—Margreta, age 18, after her boyfriend raped her

If Someone Close to You Has Been a Victim

The concern and support of loved ones are important to someone who has been raped. Recovery from rape is easier if victims know they can count on others.

You can support a rape victim. If a friend or loved one tells you she or he has been raped, you can do these things.

Believe the victim.

Listen and do not judge.

Comfort the person. Tell the victim that she or he is not to blame.

Offer to take the victim to the hospital.

Offer the victim a place to stay. Rape victims should not be left alone.

Encourage the person to go to the police or see a counselor if she or he has not already done so. However, don't pressure the victim to make decisions she or he may not be ready to make.

Help the victim find a professional counselor if this is what the victim wants.

Accept the victim's way of dealing with the rape.

Be available whenever the victim needs to talk.

Be patient and understanding. People differ in how and when they recover.

Don't fall apart with the victim. If you have trouble with your own feelings about what happened, see a counselor. Many agencies offer help to loved ones of victims.

"When my daughter first told me about the rape, I thought she was partly to blame. Then I realized that was wrong. I am glad I let her talk without passing judgment, especially when I wasn't thinking clearly."
—Harold, the father of a 19-year-old rape victim

Points to Consider

If you were a rape victim, what would you do? Why?

Why do you think it is important for a rape victim to get medical help right away?

Would you press charges against an attacker? Why or why not?

How could you help a close friend or relative who was raped?

Chapter Overview

Positive change has occurred in dealing with rape.

Males are getting more involved in rape prevention.

Many people are working to reduce violence in the media.

You can work to prevent rape.

Chapter **6**

Working to Prevent Date and Acquaintance Rape

Communities are working to increase safety. There have been many programs to reduce sexual assault. For example, courses against rape offer give-and-take communication about sexuality. In these courses, well-trained leaders focus on dating situations in new and different ways. Through role playing and other methods, members of both genders learn about how the other thinks and feels.

Governments also recognize that change needs to occur. For example, the U.S. Senate passed the Violence Against Women Act in 1994. The act provides money for better law enforcement, rape crisis centers, and shelters for battered women. It includes new and clearer definitions of crimes against females. The act allows victims of sex crimes such as rape to sue their attacker in federal court.

Males Can Prevent Rape

The Men's Rape Prevention Project (MRPP) is a group based in Washington, D.C. It works to prevent rape and other male violence. It offers education and counseling and organizes events calling for public action. The project is for males of all ages. Those who take part are concerned for mothers, sisters, friends, and other females they know.

More information about the Violence Against Women Act and about the MRPP is available on the Internet. The Useful Addresses and Internet Sites section on page 62 includes other resources.

Date and Acquaintance Rape

The kids at school were pretty excited. The principal had asked

LOU, AGE 18

them to come listen to a speaker talk about sex and rape. Lou heard a lot of the boys making rude comments about sex. He laughed right along with them. Finally, the speaker came out. The jokes continued for a while. Then the speaker talked about rape being a crime of violence. He asked the boys to think about their moms, or sisters, or girlfriends. "How would you feel if your sister was raped?" he asked. As he talked, the room grew quiet. The students were thinking about what he said.

Afterward, Lou said, "He was saying it can't only be up to women to stop rape. Men usually cause rape, so they have to help stop it, too. It really made us guys think about how we act with girls. I know I'll be looking at them in a different way."

Some experts believe that about 10 percent of people who come to a rape crisis center are male. Most of those males have been raped by other males. Females have raped males, too, but these cases are extremely rare.

Things Males Can Do

The rapist is always fully responsible for his own behavior. A male may not be able to control his desires, but he can control his actions. The following are things males can do to be more responsible for their behavior.

Believe a person when she or he says no. Don't see it as a challenge.

Never force someone to have sex with you, no matter what he or she has done.

Don't overpower someone if you are physically stronger. The victim may stop fighting back or resisting but still be unwilling to have sex. Having sex under these circumstances is rape.

Never trap someone into having sex. That is a crime.

Do not be drawn into a gang rape, no matter how others may pressure you.

If you witness a rape, stop the attacker or call the police. You may save a life.

If you pay for a date, don't expect your date to owe you sex.

If you are confused about what the other person wants, stop what you are doing and talk about it.

Don't have sex with someone who has passed out. Sex in these circumstances is rape.

Learn to compromise. A date should be comfortable and enjoyable for both people.

People Reacting to Violence in the Media

Many people believe TV, movies, music, and video games show people as stereotypes. A stereotype is an overly simple picture of a group of people. Stereotyping makes it easier not to think of the group as people. For example, parents may be stereotyped as being stupid.

Women are common targets of stereotyping. They are often stereotyped as being silly. They may be shown as things for men to use. Harmful stereotypes like this can lead people to believe that rape is okay. Fortunately, groups are working for controls and changes in these media. Letter-writing campaigns to complain about ads have had positive results. Some companies are learning that people won't accept the use of female sexuality in advertising or entertainment.

Date and Acquaintance Rape

Some women's groups have organized protests against certain kinds of popular music. These groups believe that popular songs often describe women as men's property. The groups have protested against such song lyrics in many ways. For example, Operation PUSH (People United to Save Humanity) has asked people not to buy music that puts down females.

Some female entertainers, such as Queen Latifah, perform a counter rap that is intended to be constructive. This rap does not include the violence that some rap does. It refers to females as strong individuals.

Network and cable TV channels have been asked to help reduce violence and sex in their programming. MTV, for example, is gradually becoming more strict about its music videos. In fact, it rejects one out of four because of strong violent or sexual content.

Helping the Cause

You know of ways to take care of yourself and people you care about. You also can help your community. For example, encourage community groups to raise awareness of date and acquaintance rape and other violence. Help to create alcohol- and drug-free meeting places for teens in the community. Write or call to protest programs that reinforce negative ideas about groups of people. Publicly congratulate the media when they show the realities of date rape.

Volunteering is another way to help reduce rape or raise awareness of it. For example, volunteer at a social service center that helps rape victims. You could look into answering hot line calls for people in need. Hot line volunteers refer victims to counseling services and other sources of help.

Raise awareness at your school about date and acquaintance rape. For example, you could ask your student government to sponsor a workshop on date rape. Ask a hot line or crisis center to invite rape survivors to be on a panel. Invite college or professional athletes to talk with your school about responsible sexual behavior.

Points to Consider

How might the Violence Against Women Act affect you or someone you know?

Do you think there is a difference between real life and life as shown on TV? How might this affect the way people think about other people?

Do you think stereotypes are destructive? Why or why not?

Do you think it is important for males to be involved in preventing rape? Why or why not?

Do you think there are males who see females only as objects? Why or why not?

Glossary

assault (uh-SAWLT)—violence that can cause permanent physical and emotional harm, yet that may not kill someone

boundary (BOUN-duh-ree)—a physical or emotional limit placed on something

consent (kuhn-SENT)—to agree with or give permission

counselor (KOUN-suh-lur)—a professional who is trained to listen to and help people with their problems

date rape (DAYT RAYP)—forced sexual intercourse with someone the victim knows

denial (di-NYE-uhl)—an attempt to believe that something did not happen

emotional boundary (i-MOH-shuh-nuhl BOUN-duh-ree)—the emotional closeness one person allows another; a person might allow a brother or sister to say something that would not be accepted from a stranger.

gang rape (GANG RAYP)—a rape in which more than one person attacks someone

genitals (JEN-uh-tuhlz)—sexual organs, including the vagina, clitoris, penis, and scrotum

human immunodeficiency virus (HIV) (HYOO-muhn i-MYOO-noh-di-FISH-uhn-see VYE-ruhss)—the virus that causes AIDS

physical boundary (FIZ-uh-kuhl BOUN-duh-ree)—the space a person keeps between himself or herself and another person

rape (RAYP)—unwanted sexual intercourse forced on a person

rapist (RAYP-ist)—a person who commits rape

stereotype (STER-ee-oh-tipe)—an overly simple picture of a group of people

trauma (TRAW-muh)—a severe and painful emotional shock or physical injury

violence (VYE-uh-luhnss)—words or actions that hurt people or the things they care about

Glossary

For More Information

Date Rape: The Danger Is Not From a Stranger. Northfield, MN: Life Skills Education, 1996.

Gedatus, Gus. *Stalking.* Mankato, MN: Capstone, 2000.

Gedatus, Gus. *Violence in the Media.* Mankato, MN: Capstone, 2000.

Mufson, Susan. *Straight Talk About Date Rape.* Revised edition. New York: Facts on File, 1997.

Useful Addresses and Internet Sites

Men's Rape Prevention Project
PO Box 57144
Washington, DC 20037-7144
www.mrpp.org

National Organization for Women
100 16th Street, Northwest
Suite 700
Washington, DC 20036
www.now.org

White Ribbon Campaign
365 Bloor Street East
Suite 1600
Toronto, Ontario M4W 3L4
CANADA
1-800-328-2228

Alcohol and Other Drug Education Service
www.ksu.edu/ucs/daterape.html
Information about date rape drugs, alcohol and rape, sexual assault, and tips on preventing date rape at parties

Alcohol and Women
www.glness.com/ndhs/rape.html
Information about date rape in relation to alcohol use, tips for how to handle situations in which someone is trying to force sex, and what to do if date rape occurs

National Crime Prevention Council
www.ncpc.org/10yth3.htm
Information on sexual stereotypes, what teens can do to avoid date rape, and what to do if date rape happens

Sexual Assault Information Page
www.cs.utk.edu/~bartley/saInfoPage.html
Resources for students, teachers, and community leaders, and referrals to sources of help for people affected by rape

National Youth Crisis Hotline
1-800-448-4663

Index

Index continued

Men's Rape Prevention Project
(MRPP), 52
mistaken ideas, 15, 17–19
mistrust, 26, 28
mixed messages, 34, 38
MTV, 57
myths, 9, 11, 34, 38

neighbors, 6, 40
nondating situations, 40, 41

Operation PUSH, 57

parties, 11, 39, 41
passing out, 20, 21, 55. *See also* legal
issues; unconsciousness
paying for dates, 18, 37, 55. *See also*
dating
peer pressure, 11, 55
physical effects, 23, 26–27
physical violence, 7
playing hard to get, 18. *See also* saying
no
police, 7, 16, 24, 41, 44, 47, 55. *See
also* pressing charges
power, 6
pregnancy, 26
pressing charges, 24, 29, 45. *See also*
legal issues; police

Queen Latifah, 57

rape. *See* acquaintance rape; date rape
rapists, 6–7, 8
characteristics of, 8, 18, 36, 54
consequences for, 29–30
person known to victim, 6, 8, 10,
11, 26
planning to rape, 8, 9, 10
strangers, 6, 9, 12, 26

rap music, 57
relationships, 23, 29
responsibility, 7, 15, 24, 25, 30, 53, 54,
55
Rohypnol, 21
"roofies," 21

saying no, 12, 18, 36, 38, 40, 54. *See
also* legal issues; playing hard
to get
sexual activity, 9, 11
boundaries for, 35, 37
sexual assault, 8, 44, 51
sexual effects, 27–28
sexually suggestive comments, 34, 40
sexually transmitted diseases, 26
sleeping problems, 27
social workers, 45
stereotypes, 56
stomachaches, 27
suicide, 43
support groups, 25
supporting rape victims, 26, 28, 45,
46–48

talking. *See* communication
television, 57, 58
therapy, 28, 43
trapping dates, 9, 10, 55. *See also*
dating; legal issues

unconsciousness, 10, 20, 21. *See also*
legal issues; passing out
unreported rape, 7–8

victims, definition of, 15
Violence Against Women Act, 52
volunteering, 58

weapons, 7